# What Is Media?

## Elizabeth Anderson Lopez

## Reader Consultants

**Cheryl Norman Lane, M.A.Ed.**
*Classroom Teacher*
Chino Valley Unified School District

**Jennifer M. Lopez, M.S.Ed., NBCT**
*Teacher Specialist—History/Social Studies*
Norfolk Public Schools

## iCivics Consultants

**Emma Humphries, Ph.D.**
*Chief Education Officer*

**Taylor Davis, M.T.**
*Director of Curriculum and Content*

**Natacha Scott, MAT**
*Director of Educator Engagement*

## Publishing Credits

Rachelle Cracchiolo, M.S.Ed., *Publisher*
Emily R. Smith, M.A.Ed., *VP of Content Development*
Véronique Bos, *Creative Director*
Dona Herweck Rice, *Senior Content Manager*
Dani Neiley, *Associate Content Specialist*
Fabiola Sepulveda, *Series Designer*

**Image Credits:** p.5 southerlycourse/iStock; p.6 Songquan Deng/Shutterstock; p.10 Andrey Bayda/Shutterstock; p.14 Kathy deWitt/Alamy; p.15 (bottom), p.18 Walter Mladina; p.19 (bottom) Sunshine Seeds/Shutterstock; p.21 Kena Betancur/AFP via Getty Images; p.22 STF/AFP via Getty Images; p.23 Creative Touch Imaging Ltd./NurPhoto via Getty Images; p.27 Richard Levine/Alamy; all other images from iStock and/or Shutterstock

## Library of Congress Cataloging-in-Publication Data

Names: Lopez, Elizabeth Anderson, author.
Title: What is media? / Elizabeth Anderson Lopez.
Description: Huntington Beach, CA : Teacher Created Materials, [2021] |
  Series: iCivics | Includes index. | Audience: Grades 2-3. | Summary:
  "The media is a great tool to learn about all sorts of things. There are
  newspapers, magazines, online sources and more. But not everything you
  read or hear is true. Learn how to be like a detective and tell facts
  from opinions!"-- Provided by publisher.
Identifiers: LCCN 2020016295 (print) | LCCN 2020016296 (ebook) | ISBN
  9781087605173 (paperback) | ISBN 9781087619415 (ebook)
Subjects: LCSH: Mass media--Juvenile literature. | Media literacy--Juvenile
  literature. | Journalism--Juvenile literature. | Press and
  politics--Juvenile literature.
Classification: LCC P91.2 .L67 2021 (print) | LCC P91.2 (ebook) | DDC
  302.23--dc23
LC record available at https://lccn.loc.gov/2020016295
LC ebook record available at https://lccn.loc.gov/2020016296

5482 Argosy Avenue
Huntington Beach, CA 92649-1039
www.tcmpub.com

**ISBN 978-1-0876-0517-3**
© 2022 Teacher Created Materials, Inc.

# Table of Contents

# What Is Media?

You learn many things at school, but that is not the only way to learn. You can learn from watching TV or reading articles online. You might read magazines or newspapers. They make it easy to stay up-to-date with news. Those sources are known as *media*. They report on sports, entertainment, world events, and lots of other topics.

People read and watch the news.

The media plays an important role in our freedoms as citizens. We expect to read truthful stories. In return, we must learn to judge what we read. We have to be able to tell facts from opinions. It can be a tough job! There is a famous saying that goes: "You can't believe everything you read." It is up to the reader to decide.

Jump into Fiction

# Yoli's Lesson

Yoli and her dad were in the kitchen when she heard the theme music for *Hughes on News*. She wanted to be a reporter, and the song made her smile.

"Good evening, I'm George Hughes," the man on the screen began. "Mayor Timmons should be fired! He isn't doing enough to help the shelter find homes for dogs and cats. He doesn't like animals."

Yoli stopped what she was doing, confused. "Dad," Yoli began. "Mr. Hughes clearly doesn't like the mayor. I thought reporters were supposed to stick to the facts."

Yoli's dad smiled. "You're right," he tells her. "But there are different kinds of reporters. George Hughes's show is all about his opinions. You write articles for the school website, right? As a columnist, you tell students what you think about different topics. Hughes is kind of like that."

Yoli thought about what her dad said. But she was still confused. Yoli's dad turned on his tablet and went to a few websites about the animal shelter. "The city website says it gave less money to the animal shelter this year than last year," Yoli's dad reads aloud. "That means Hughes is right," Yoli replies.

City Website

ABOUT | SERVICES | SOLUTIONS | SUPPORT | CONTACTS

Call Us : +12 34 567 89

HOME | SITEMAP | CONTACT | PURCHASE

# Funding for Local Shelter Cut

After months of back and forth, next year's city budget has been finalized. Funding for a few programs, including the Main Street Animal Shelter, has been cut. Mayor Timmons announced the budget cuts yesterday during the monthly town hall meeting. He apologized but called the budget cuts "necessary."

"Not exactly," her dad says. "The fact that they got less money is a fact. The mayor not wanting to help animals is an opinion. Hughes said it's the mayor's fault. But there may be other reasons. Can you think of some?"

"Um...maybe the mayor isn't the only one who decides how money should be spent?"

"That's true," Yoli's dad agrees. "Hughes is sharing news, but he's also sharing his opinion. Being able to tell fact from opinion is important."

Back to Nonfiction

# Different Kinds of Media

Media is everywhere. You may see an advertisement as you board a city bus. Or, you may see a billboard as you drive on a highway. Even while at home, there are many types of media you may see. One of the most common forms of media people encounter is through television.

Times Square
in New York City

People may have access to hundreds of TV shows at any given time. These shows cover lots of different topics. Some shows are fiction, such as cartoons. Some shows are nonfiction, such as the news.

A fictional TV show may have an **agenda**. That means the show has a specific message. This message might be the value of sports teams. Or, the message might be that bullying is not okay. Whatever the message, most fictional TV shows have **biases**.

## Black and White

Shows weren't always in color like you see them today. All shows used to be in black and white. Color TV sets weren't invented until the early 1950s.

Nonfiction shows, such as news programs, are important. They help people learn about the world around them. The news is supposed to tell people facts. Just like fictional shows, though, news programs can have biases. Sometimes, bias is revealed by what the news does *not* show.

Think **and** Talk

How do you or your family learn about the news?

KARA JONES

JULIE SIMMS

LIVE NEWS FROM CITY HALL

24 LIVE NEWS

**City Council Candidates**

Suppose there are three people running for city council. Their names are Kara, Julie, and Jaime. The news reporter talks to Kara and Julie for 20 minutes each. He does not talk to Jaime at all. This could mean a few things. Maybe the reporter doesn't support Jaime for city council. Or, maybe Jaime was not available. It is the viewers' job to notice that the three people weren't treated the same. Viewers might have to do research to learn why. If there was a bias, viewers can make a note of that if watching the program in the future.

Biases can be unfair. In the case of the city council interviews, there could have been a bias. Maybe Jaime wanted to change a law that would affect the TV station. Without Jaime present, it appears that the TV station has a bias. However, it is always worth the time to check the facts.

In addition to TV, people get news from other forms of media. Newspapers and magazines are part of **print media**. They both report on news. Sometimes, magazines will have one main focus, such as sports or cooking. Those articles can still be news, though. When a team wins a big game, for instance, that is both news *and* sports. Newspapers tend to have lots of sections. The main focus in a newspaper is current events. But if there is bias, it can show in any or all of the sections.

# It's the Best!

Some companies send out **press releases** for their new products. Press releases are meant to give information. Editors have to make sure the releases include facts, not opinions, about the products. A fact about a bike might be that it has a leather seat. An opinion is that it's the most comfortable seat in the world.

PRESS RELEASE
Speedster Beach Cruiser Bike!

• Padded leather seat for maximum comfort
• Thick tires can roll over road debris
• Comfortable easy-grip handlebars

**Showbiz Nightingale**
New tricks with old songs **Page 3**

**Childcare: New Theory**
How to keep kids happier **Page 6**

**Secret of Happiness**
Wives no longer desperate **Page 8**

## The Journal
TUESDAY

# BIG NEWS!

'So it seems we now have a choice'

NASA Astronauts Launch in Historic Test Flight

**Local Animal Shelter Gets Big Donation**

A new approach to computing....

**International Markets Shrug Off Damage Caused by Storm**

The storm's fury caused millions of dollars in damage.

...from the people with new ideas.

The biggest news of the day is featured on the top half of the front page "above the fold."

15

Most stories in print media have bylines. A *byline* is the name of the author. There is one kind of story, though, that does not get a byline. That story is called an *editorial*. An editorial tells the opinion of the newspaper or magazine. This is often done for big events. One example is an election. Writers for magazines or newspapers will write about who they think should win and why.

In print media, there are often advertisements that look just like articles. Companies want people to think the story was written *about* them. But it was really written *by* them. The goal is to trick readers. This makes opinions look like facts. There are laws to help readers. Companies have to use words that tell readers that these pieces are ads. They might write "sponsored" on the ad. They might write "paid ad." Sometimes, though, those words are easy to miss.

## Digital Ads

The law on sponsored ads does not only apply to print media. It also applies to things such as social media. **Influencers** have to say when they got paid for posts. They often do this through hashtags, such as #ad or #spon.

# The Daily News

First Edition

Monday, March 8, 2020

## Broken Bridges; Broken Promises

**OPINION**

When voters elected the unqualified and inexperienced Mayor Greene last fall, he promised to fund the repairs of the community's crumbling bridges. Nearly a year into his term and not a single brick has been replaced.

I recently spoke with Jaime Martinez, the founder of locally owned Martinez Construction. Martinez Construction is often the mayor's office's first choice for quick, local jobs. Mr. Martinez confirmed to me that no one from the mayor's office has reached out for a repair quote. Mr. Martinez confirmed many residents' fears that if they don't fix the bridges soon, they will have to wait until the spring thaw as the snowy ground will be too hard to dig into.

The Sixth Street Bridge made headlines across the state last summer when it suddenly collapsed. Mayor Greene made bridge repairs a key part of his campaign's platform, which won many voters to his side. Now, his campaign motto of "Better Bridges for a Better Future" seems to be a relic of the past. Mayor Greene's office refused to comment on his bridge blunder.

*Sixth Street Bridge repairs*

## New Study Gives Hope

**By Valeria Fabregas**

A new report out of Eastvale University shows that people feel less stress when they speak to therapists on a regular basis. The study followed a group of two hundred 15–50 year olds for a year. Researchers asked

*Study/see page 10*

People get information from lots of other forms of media too.  Many people read news online.  Readers have to be **critical** of what they read online.  Is a story true?  Are there sources to back it up?  Is there bias?  Remember that anyone can post online.  People may not fact-check things before they share them.

A lot of people get news from the radio.  One in four American adults say they often get news that way.  Radio show hosts might talk about new music that is coming out.  Or, they might talk about current events.  Those shows are often called "talk radio."  Radio shows can have biases too.

Books are also a form of media.  They are one of the oldest too!  Nonfiction books are full of facts.  They may also have the authors' opinions.  That is another form of bias.

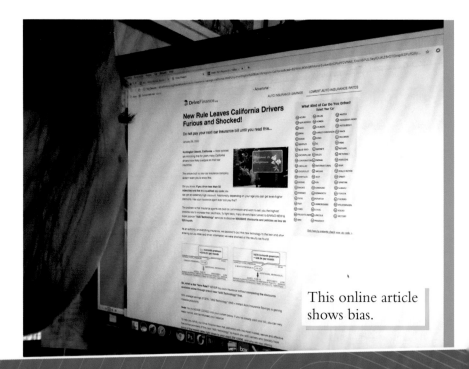

This online article shows bias.

## ABCs of the FCC

There is a group in the government that oversees TV and radio shows. The group is called the Federal Communications Commission, or the FCC. It makes sure that **broadcasts** follow the rules. But the law says that the FCC can't block a show's point of view.

Hosts of radio talk shows such as these may have biases.

# Media and Democracy

When our nation was founded, people thought about what was important. The **Founders** knew that the nation had to have a free press. A *free press* means that news reporting is free from the government's influence. The press cannot be controlled or silenced for political reasons. The press has the right to report on what they want. Sometimes, people in power may not like what the press says. Even then, they cannot influence the free press.

The Founders discuss the new nation.

The Founders thought a free press was so important that they put it in the Bill of Rights. It is in the First **Amendment**. That amendment also says that people have free speech. It says they can practice any religion too.

## In the Words of Jefferson

One of the nation's Founders was Thomas Jefferson. He was a key supporter of a free press. He once said, "Our liberty depends on the freedom of the press." He said that a free press "cannot be limited without being lost."

People in the United States are lucky. There are lots of countries that don't have a free press. The people in charge tell the media what to say. They can use the media to change how people think. For instance, imagine that most people in a country do not support a new law. The leader can use the media to lie. They can say that most people like the new law. This might convince other people to support the law too. When reporters in those countries do not report what the government wants, they can get in serious trouble.

Some countries **censor** the internet. This means they block certain websites. Citizens can't learn what they want. The government decides what people can and cannot see. This is not how a democracy works. Those countries often have only a few people in charge.

This website is blocked in China.

## Free Press Limits

A free press does have some limits. For example, a writer cannot spread lies that will hurt a person's reputation. This is called *libel*, and it is against the law.

# FreeInternet4IRAN

Don't be scared

We Are All Together

This man asks for an uncensored internet.

The media has responsibilities. So does the public. People need to keep the media in check. They can do this by learning how to spot bias.

The best way to see bias is to look at the source of the information. Suppose there was a **study** that said soda was a healthy drink. If a soda company had done the study, the results might show bias. The study might have less bias if a **third-party** group had done it. In this case, a third-party group would be a group that doesn't sell soda.

## New Study Confirms Soda Is Healthy for You

A recent study proves the benefits of drinking soda. In addition to providing the calories needed for your body to function properly, the high water levels in soft drinks are essential for proper nutrition. With all these health benefits, soda has now been proven to be much more beneficial than we've been led to believe.

**Regular Soda**

water
other ingredients

**Diet Soda**

water
other ingredients

*Study paid for by the Sunshine Soda Company.*

Bias can be anywhere. Suppose an influencer shares a post about how great her shoes are for skateboarding. What if the shoe company paid her to write about it? That's bias too!

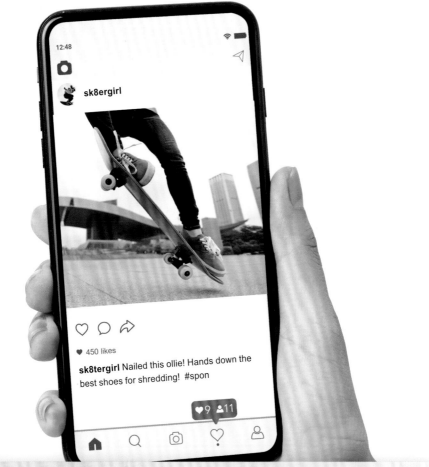

# Part of the Solution

There are lots of media jobs that people can have. Some people are reporters or editors. Some people are fact-checkers or lawyers. These jobs are needed in all kinds of media.

People can share posts or articles online quickly and easily. Online readers can do their part by looking up the facts first. It is easy to check facts before sharing them. That can help to stop spreading stories that aren't true.

Readers can point out when they see false information. They can comment on articles. Or, they can write letters to editors. This can help inspire people to make up their own minds.

Some social media platforms have added fact-checking to posts.

This girl supports a free press.

People who want to support a free press can speak out. Some people might disagree with the way media reports on a leader or a topic, but they still support a free press. When people defend the press, it doesn't mean they agree with what was said. Standing up for a free press is a way to stand up for democracy!

## In the Words of Hall

Evelyn Beatrice Hall was an English author. She wrote, "I disapprove of what you say, but I will defend to the death your right to say it." People who support free speech and free press use this quote often.

# Media Matters

People get information from different media sources every day. They read trending news online. They flip through magazines. They listen to the radio. It's in their homes and out in the world. Having a free press is important. It was a key part of the founding of the country. It still helps form the groundwork of a democracy.

Sometimes, though, the media can be misleading. It is up to the readers and listeners to determine fact from opinion. It is up to them to spot bias. It can be hard work, but it is necessary.

Media matters! So does your role in it. Media can help you learn about current events. It can even help you understand your role in the world.

## Think and Talk

What are some things in this book that should be fact-checked?

# Glossary

**agenda**—a plan to affect other people's thoughts or behavior

**amendment**—a change made to a law or legal document

**biases**—beliefs that some ideas and people are better than others, which often results in treating some topics or people unfairly

**broadcasts**—television or radio programs

**censor**—to remove things that are considered to be immoral, harmful, or offensive

**critical**—using careful judgment about the good and bad parts of something

**Founders**—the people who played an important role in creating the U.S. government

**influencers**—people who create interest in things by posting about them on social media

**press releases**—official statements that give information to media outlets

**print media**—a form of communication delivered through printing, such as newspapers, banners, magazines, journals, and books

**study**—an organized experiment that is done to learn more about a topic

**third-party**—refers to a person or group who is involved in something but is not one of the main groups affected by it

# Index

# Civics in Action

The media can be a great source for learning something new. But people should be critical of what they learn. Maybe not everything they read is fact. Maybe the report or show has bias. It is up to citizens to be media savvy.

1.  Read or listen to a news report.

2.  Think about the information.

3.  Check the report for any opinions or biases.

4.  Find facts that should be fact-checked.

5.  Write a report of your own on the topic. Only include facts. Do not include your biases.